CHANCE THE RAPPER

INDEPENDENT INNOVATOR

BY DIANE BAILEY

Essential Library

An Imprint of Abdo Publishing
abdopublishing.com

ABDOPUBLISHING.COM

Published by Abdo Publishing, a division of ABDO, PO Box 398166, Minneapolis, Minnesota 55439. Copyright © 2018 by Abdo Consulting Group, Inc. International copyrights reserved in all countries. No part of this book may be reproduced in any form without written permission from the publisher. Essential Library™ is a trademark and logo of Abdo Publishing.

Printed in the United States of America, North Mankato, Minnesota
102017
012018

Cover Photo: David Jensen/PA Wire URN:29528617/AP Images
Interior Photos: Mathieu Bitton/Rex Features/Shutterstock Images, 4; Jeff Kravitz/
FilmMagic, Inc/Getty Images, 7; Maria Sbytova/Shutterstock Images, 10–11;
Jamie Lamor Thompson/Shutterstock Images, 12; Emma McIntyre/Getty Images
Entertainment/Getty Images, 14–15; Cliff Schiappa/AP Images, 19; Daniel Boczarski/
Getty Images Entertainment/Getty Images, 22–23; Kathy Hutchins/Shutterstock
Images, 25, 51; Tim Mosenfelder/Getty Images Entertainment/Getty Images, 27;
Robb D. Cohen/RobbsPhotos/Invision/AP Images, 28; Kevin Winter/ Getty Images
Entertainment/Getty Images, 33; Debby Wong/Shutterstock Images, 36–37;
Goodgroves/Rex Features/AP Images, 38; Christian Bertrand/Shutterstock Images,
43; Felipe Frazao/Shutterstock Images, 44–45; Robb D. Cohen/Invision/AP Images,
47, 56; Matt Sayles/Invision/AP Images, 48, 64, 66, 86; Charles Rex Arbogast/AP
Images, 52, 62–63, 84–85; Timothy Hiatt/ Getty Images Entertainment/Getty
Images, 55; Paul Natkin/Archive Photos/Getty Images, 60–61; Chris Pizzello/
Invision/AP Images, 71; PictureGroup/Sipa USA/Newscom, 75; Nam Y. Huh/
AP Images, 76; Papa Bravo/Shutterstock Images, 81; Paul Morigi/Getty Images
Entertainment/Getty Images, 82; Cindy Barrymore/Rex Features/AP Images, 90–91;
Rob Grabowski/Invision/AP Images, 94–95; Joel Ryan/Invision/AP Images, 97

Editor: Brenda Haugen
Series Designer: Laura Polzin

PUBLISHER'S CATALOGING-IN-PUBLICATION DATA

Names: Bailey, Diane, author.
Title: Chance the Rapper: independent innovator / by Diane Bailey.
Other titles: Independent innovator
Description: Minneapolis, Minnesota : Abdo Publishing, 2018. | Series: Hip-hop
    artists |
Includes online resources and index.
Identifiers: LCCN 2017946867 | ISBN 9781532113253 (lib.bdg.) | ISBN 9781532152139
    (ebook)
Subjects: LCSH: Chance the Rapper (Chancellor Bennett), 1993-.--Juvenile
    literature. | Rap musicians--United States--Biography--Juvenile literature. |
    Rap (Music)--Juvenile literature.
Classification: DDC 782.421649 [B]--dc23
LC record available at https://lccn.loc.gov/2017946867

CONTENTS

Chapter ONE

A FATEFUL SUMMER

During the summer of 2011, Chancelor "Chance" Bennett was 18 years old, freshly graduated from high school, and ready to take charge of his life. He liked growing up in West Chatham, a neighborhood on the South Side of Chicago, Illinois, but now he looked forward to the next step. He wanted to put school behind him. He did not excel at academics, and his grades reflected that. His low grades probably stemmed partly from attention deficit hyperactivity disorder (ADHD), a condition that makes it difficult to concentrate. In addition, he simply did not have much interest in school.

Chance had a particularly rocky time during his senior year of high school. After getting caught smoking marijuana in an alley one morning before school, Chance was arrested, and school administrators suspended him for two weeks. His parents did not approve of his

A major turning point in Chance's life in 2011 put him on the path to his current success.

behavior, but things at school did not improve much after the suspension. When final exams rolled around, Chance skipped one of his tests so he could go to band practice. That meant he was not able to graduate on time, although he later got his diploma.

Chance did not consider himself college material, but his father, Ken, saw things differently. Ken was adamant that Chance continue his education. The elder Bennett had made a career in government and community service and hoped his son would follow in his footsteps. He thought Chance might run for a political office someday. But Chance had no interest in getting a job in politics. He had radically different plans. He wanted to pursue a career as a rap musician, as his idol Kanye West had done. Ken disapproved of his son's choice, but Chance held firm to his dream. Although he had always respected his father and saw him as a role model, Chance was 18 and felt ready to make his own decisions. The disagreement caused a rift in their relationship, and they stopped speaking to each other.

During his suspension from school, Chance had started a new music project. He would later name it *10 Day*, since he began working on it during the two weeks he was suspended. The tracks were about high

Chance's father, Ken, and mother, Lisa, were not convinced a career in rap was the best option for their son.

school life—everything from the prom to Spanish class. After finishing high school, he continued working on the project.

Chance had been producing mixtapes for several years. However, making music on the side in high school was one thing. Turning it into a career was another.

Chance wanted to devote his future to music, but he wondered whether his dad had a good point about continuing his education. Still young and unsure of his future, Chance enrolled in Harold Washington College, a neighborhood community college, but he soon regretted the decision. He dropped out after only a week. As fall approached, Chance seemed to be at a crossroads. Should he take a traditional path or follow his dream? The answer was about to become clear to him.

One night in early September 2011, Chance was out with friends in Lincoln Park, a Chicago neighborhood several miles from his home. What began as an evening of fun ended in tragedy. Chance's friend Rodney Kyles, who also was a rapper, was hoping to attend a house party. Instead, he ended up in a fight.

WHAT IS A MIXTAPE?

Chance's recordings are often referred to as albums, but he prefers to use the word *mixtapes*. When cassette tapes were popular in the 1980s, people often made tapes of songs that did not necessarily fit together—a mixtape. Today the term is used in hip-hop music to describe a compilation of songs that may have only a loose common thread or be less polished than a formal studio release. Artists often use these informal releases as a way to build their fan bases, and they are usually free.

Within just a few minutes, the violence turned worse. Kyles, 19, was stabbed multiple times. Chance watched the whole thing.

Kyles was rushed to the hospital, but it was too late to save his life. Chance was badly shaken. Although it was the middle of the night and he had not spoken to his father in months, Chance called him. Chance knew his dad would come get him no matter what.

When his dad got to the hospital, Chance still had Kyles's blood on his shirt. It served as a stark reminder of what he had been through—and what he had escaped. That night was a turning point for both Chance and his dad. Both of

REMEMBERING ROD

Witnessing the death of Rodney Kyles was incredibly difficult for Chance. Kyles was only 19 when he was murdered. When Chance turned 20, in 2013, he was struck by the fact that he was now older than his friend had been when he died. One way Chance dealt with his grief was by rapping about it. Several of his songs include references to the incident. In the track "Acid Rain," from the tape *Acid Rap*, Chance reveals how the event is always on his mind: "I seen it happen, I seen it happen, I see it always."[1]

"My dad taught me to work hard and my mom taught me to work for myself. So now I work for myself really hard."[2]
—*Chance the Rapper, in an interview with Katie Couric, February 28, 2017*

His friend's death in Lincoln Park was the catalyst for Chance's career.

them realized that things could have gone differently that night. It could have been Chance in the fight. It could have been Chance who never came home. Grateful his son was

still alive, Ken resolved to accept Chance's decisions. He gave Chance his blessing to try to make it as a rapper.

Chance also took a hard look at his life and his future. He vowed to make every day count. After Kyles's death,

Chance became more focused and serious. "It was just a wake up call, kind of like, I'm young and I could definitely die in Chicago," he said later in an interview with *HipHopDX*. "It's not guaranteed that I'm going to be able to live a full day."[3] Chance began showing up to the studio every day to record tracks and shoot videos, and he put more energy into promoting himself with live shows. "It just became more of a career for me and less of a hobby," he said.[4]

While Kyles's death had been a staggering blow, Chance refused to let it—or any other event—hold him back. He would let his experiences guide him, but they would not paralyze him. Now, with his father's blessing, Chance could chase his dream.

A KID FROM CHICAGO

When Chancelor Bennett was born, on April 16, 1993, Chicago's music scene was being reborn. Hip-hop had started two decades earlier in New York City, but now, Chicago was its new hot spot. Just the year before, rapper Common Sense (now known just as Common) had released his first album, *Can I Borrow a Dollar?* Another local, Tung Twista (shortened now to Twista) earned a Guinness World Record for uttering the most syllables in a minute.

Chance and his brother, Taylor Bennett, *left*, have both made careers in the music industry.

15

Along with hip-hop, Chicago served as a hotbed for jazz, soul, rock and roll, and electronic music. Chance spent his childhood and teen years surrounded by this vibrant musical environment, and it turned him into who he is today.

GROWING UP ON THE SOUTH SIDE

Chance grew up in West Chatham, a neighborhood on Chicago's South Side. The South Side has a storied reputation. Notorious gangster Al Capone ruled the area in the 1920s, and since then it has gained a reputation as a dangerous, violent place. However, that is only one view of the South Side. Although parts of the area are poor and crime-ridden, many others are not. Chance was raised in a middle-class neighborhood, and his family has a long history there. His family owned the same house on 79th Street for generations.

Chance's father, Ken, worked for the mayor and later for the city's tourism department. For a time, Ken worked for Illinois senator Barack Obama, who would eventually become president of the United States. Chance's mother, Lisa, was employed in the state attorney general's office. Chance also has a younger brother, Taylor Bennett, who was born in 1996.

Chance had a pretty normal upbringing. As a child, he carried a *Rugrats* lunch box and read the Harry Potter books. He caught lightning bugs on steamy summer evenings and avoided eating his vegetables.

Community living was a big part of his childhood. In his neighborhood, it seemed everyone was only one person away from knowing everyone else. If you did not know someone personally, then you probably at least knew her cousin, or that was how it felt. Ken ran the neighborhood block association, and he expected Chance to be a good neighbor. If an elderly neighbor needed help with the trash or shoveling snow, young Chance found himself volunteered for the chore. Ken instilled a sense of community responsibility that Chance carries today.

FAMILY TIES

No matter how famous he gets, Taylor Bennett will always be Chance's little brother, and Taylor knows it. The two grew up rapping together, and it comes as no surprise that both brothers picked rapping as a career. Chance shot to stardom first, but Taylor boasts a distinct style of his own and a growing fan base to go with it. He released his first album, *Broad Shoulders*, in 2015. He followed it up with *Restoration of an American Idol* in 2017. The brothers like to use their family ties when possible. Chance makes vocal appearances on both of his brother's releases. He is featured in the title track of *Broad Shoulders* and on *Idol*'s "Grown Up Fairy Tales."

"My personality and my character and my understanding of how I respond to people and how I work with people and how I present my opinions—I get that from my dad," Chance said in an interview with the magazine *GQ*.[1]

Another big part of his childhood was church. Chance spent most of his Sundays and summers at the Covenant Faith Church of God, a primarily black church where his grandmother had started a church camp for kids in the early 1970s. From great music to early romances, church was where Chance learned about life.

GETTING STARTED

Chance showed his love of performing at an early age. At his preschool graduation, Chance staged a skit in which he dressed up as the King of Pop, Michael Jackson. Chance wore dark glasses, a leather jacket, and Jackson's trademark white glove.

In 2001, by age eight, Chance's affinity for music and entertainment had gelled into a specific goal. Chance knew he wanted to be a rapper when he grew up. He liked to watch *Def Poetry*, a television show hosted by rapper Mos Def that showcased spoken-word performers. He also found he enjoyed poetry and rhyming. In the fourth grade, Chance visited his grandmother, and she handed

Chance studied pop icon Michael Jackson to learn how to perform live.

him a notebook. Chance used it to write a poem. In fifth grade, just before he turned 11 in 2004, Chance bought his first rap album, Kanye West's *The College Dropout*. West became Chance's idol.

In 2007, at 14 years old, Chance jumped at his first opportunity to try recording, at a studio where one of his cousins worked. Chance went with a couple of friends to lay down vocals on top of instrumentals performed by West. Hearing his own voice hooked Chance even more on being a rapper. The next year he started his own rap group, Instrumentality, with his best friend, Justin. Chance also joined a youth performance program called YouMedia, as well as the group Young Chicago Authors. Through those groups, aspiring artists could practice performing.

One of Chance's early struggles was not with writing his songs—it was with remembering them. Mike Hawkins, an established spoken-word artist who worked with YouMedia, told Chance that if he could not remember the words to his own songs while he was performing, he would lose fans. After the warning, Hawkins said, he never heard Chance mess up again.

Meanwhile, Chance made mixtapes at home and handed them out at school and on the streets. Friendly, energetic, and outgoing, Chance was the textbook image of an extrovert. Getting people to listen to him talk about his music—much less take the time to listen to it—proved challenging. But Chance had a fun, easygoing way about him, and if he held out the headphones long enough, people eventually would put them on and check out what was on the tapes. If they liked his music, they walked away with a complimentary CD.

"I didn't know the back history; I just felt the energy. Immediately there was something that was relatable to the younger kids and the older people."[2]
—Alex Fruchter, cofounder of Chicago record label Closed Sessions

Giving his music away for free was one thing—but the CDs themselves cost money. Financially speaking, it was not the best business decision, and Chance's dad told him as much. But Chance did not want any barriers to people hearing his music. He wanted to reach as many people as possible, and the best way to do that was to distribute his music for free.

Chance practiced performing through programs such as Young Chicago Authors and YouMedia.

HIGH SCHOOL TROUBLE

Chance grew up in a loving, supportive family. His parents strove to give him good opportunities, such as attending the well-regarded private high school Jones College Prep. Although Chance recognized that he was being offered a good education, taking on a tough academic schedule was not a good fit for him. He was more interested in poetry and music than grades and good behavior.

Chance often ended up In trouble for minor infractions. For example, it was against the rules to wear a baseball cap at school, but Chance did it anyway. One by one, his caps were confiscated, ending up in a box in the school office with other contraband. At the end of the year, the administrators pulled out a few caps and gave them back to their rightful owners. The rest of the box's contents went to Chance—

Chance could have gone in a bad direction after his arrest but instead chose a positive path.

MEET AND GREET

Chance never wanted to be a politician—but he might have been good at it. When he was starting out and distributing his music, Chance instinctively understood that it was important to engage his audience. In the days before he had a strong social media presence, Chance used old-fashioned ways to interact with people: handshakes and conversations. Armed with mixtapes and pamphlets promoting his events, Chance hung out on college campuses trying to woo fans. The pitch started before his audience ever heard a word or a note of his music. He tried to talk to each person for at least four minutes before turning the conversation to rap. Then—with luck—the person would already be hooked.

all the remaining hats belonged to him.

During his senior year, Chance found himself in more serious trouble when police caught him smoking marijuana one morning near his school. Chance was arrested, and school authorities disciplined him by imposing a ten-day suspension.

The suspension came shortly before spring break, so the timing meant that Chance actually had three weeks when he was not in school. Some kids might have used the extended break to catch up on sleep or zone out on video games, but Chance decided to make better use of his time. With a transcript full of poor grades

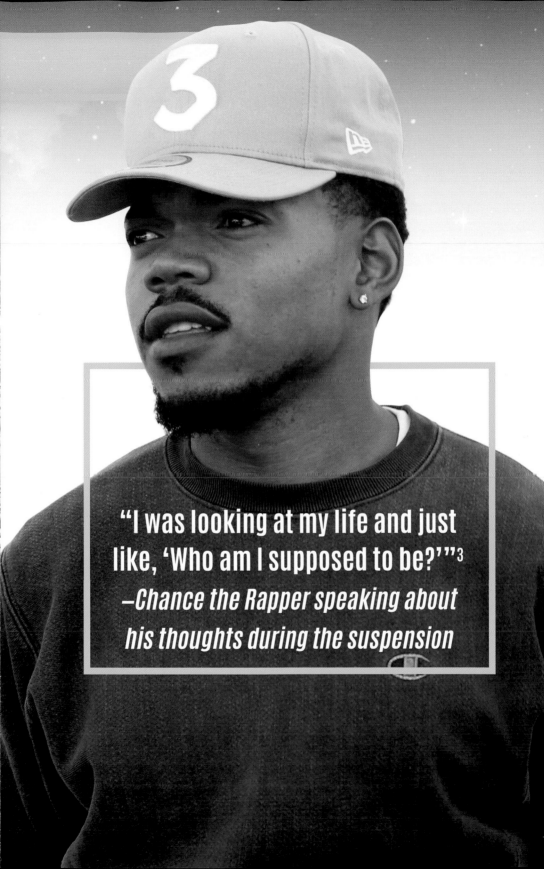

"I was looking at my life and just like, 'Who am I supposed to be?'"[3] –Chance the Rapper speaking about his thoughts during the suspension

Kanye West's *The College Dropout* was Chance's first rap album.

and even his graduation in jeopardy at that point, Chance knew it was time to start making a plan.

Rather than treat his suspension as a vacation, Chance went to work on a new project. He wrote lyrics, started laying down tracks, and began calling himself Chance the Rapper. Because he started it during his suspension, he eventually called the mixtape *10 Day*. It was about much more than a couple of weeks of high school, though. It was Chance's launch to a bigger career.

GAINING SPECIAL ATTENTION

As a teen, Chance entered a contest called "Write a Song for Chicago." His submission was called "Beddy Bye." Mike Hawkins, a Chicago artist who was one of Chance's mentors, called the song one of the best he had ever heard about Chicago— and not just from a young artist. The song earned Chance second place in the contest. It also caught the attention of Chicago's mayor, Richard Daley. When Daley paid a visit to the YouMedia space where Chance was performing, he made a point of listening to Chance's song.

BREAKTHROUGH

By the fall of 2011, Chance was ready to turn the rough tracks he had begun during the last few months into complete raps for *10 Day*. He documented the exact length of his suspension in the track "14,400 Minutes" and declared that he did not care about failing math class in "Windows," the first single off the mixtape. The lyrics of "Prom Night" reminded his teachers that they had discouraged his interest in rap—and yet here he stood, succeeding at it. The whole tape was a statement, proving himself to the people who doubted him. He was showing them he could be successful.

A YEAR FOR *10 DAY*

Chance's family and friends came together to support him as the tape came together. Fellow rapper L-Boogie of THEMPeople let Chance use his recording studio for free. Kevin Coval, a notable hip-hop poet in Chicago, helped Chance set up performances that brought in cash to help pay for living expenses, such as food and transportation.

Chance's early performances helped him gain fans.

LEAD ON

"Lead Never Follow." That is the slogan of Leaders 1354, a Chicago clothing store that specializes in stylish streetwear, including hoodies and sneakers. Chance's dad set up a performance there for his son one afternoon. Ken also invited a guest, Pat Corcoran, a Chicagoan who was immersed in the city's music scene as a blogger and promoter. Corcoran was so impressed with Chance's performance that he dropped out of college to become the rapper's manager. Since then, Corcoran has taken the lead on making Chance a star.

Chance's dad wanted him to get his rap career off the ground within one year, so he jumped in to help his son succeed. Ken arranged a show at the clothing store Leaders 1354 in downtown Chicago that drew so much interest that Chance had to repeat the event to fit everyone in.

Chance also got the opportunity to work with pros in the business, including fellow Chicago rappers Vic Mensa, Chuck Inglish of the Cool Kids, and the Blended Babies. It took a year to get the mixtape right, but Chance wasn't in a hurry. It would drop when it was ready—when *he* was ready. Meanwhile, he stoked his fans' interest by releasing a couple of teaser songs and by performing at South by Southwest, a well-known arts festival held in Austin, Texas.

10 Day was finally released in April 2012, and it proved worth the wait. Chance had worked to make a name for himself on the local scene, and the sounds on *10 Day* solidified his reputation. Although he had recorded physical CDs for some of his earlier music, this time Chance opted to go high-tech. In addition to the CDs Chance handed out on the streets, the mixtape was available to stream or download from the Internet. That meant fans did not have to run into Chance personally or borrow a CD from a friend—it was available instantly. And it was almost instantly successful, quickly racking up approximately 400,000 downloads on a music-sharing site.[1]

Something had changed with this mixtape. Chance had made other mixtapes, but this one was more thought-out and professional. The music community noticed. Chance started being compared to some of the greats in the rap world: Common, Kanye West, and Eminem. He received

SOUTH BY SOUTHWEST

In the 1980s, the city of Austin, Texas, was known for its quirky culture and energetic music scene. To help promote the city, four Austinites came up with the idea of having a festival to showcase musicians and bring in industry professionals to hear them. The first event, held in 1987, drew 700 people and featured 200 bands. By the time Chance first performed at the festival's 25-year anniversary in 2012, the event had grown tremendously. Thousands of bands perform and tens of thousands of participants attend the festival, which also highlights movies, interactive media, and new technology.

> "It's not about the music being free. It's about how it is displayed and made accessible and about artistic power. It was always about the artist-to-fan relationship."[2]
>
> —*Chance the Rapper*

attention from both the local Chicago music scene and the national one. Even *Forbes*, a magazine best known for appealing to wealthy businesspeople, recommended *10 Day* on its list of "Cheap Tunes."

ON THE RADAR

As Chance became more well-known, important people in the music industry became interested in him. Representatives from record labels heard about the young rapper and checked him out. They liked what they heard—and Chance had the fans to prove he was the real deal. Offers came in to sign him to a major deal.

Signing with a label is a big step in an artist's career. Major labels control the production and distribution of most popular music. They have the money and connections to launch and promote careers. But there are potential pitfalls. These companies not only take a big chunk of the profits but may also curtail the creativity of their artists. They may dictate who an artist can work with, what music is released and when, and how much it will cost. And if an artist does not perform as well as hoped, the label may drop him or her.

Signing with a label was a big decision, so Chance bided his time. He says he came close to making a deal with the music company Sony, but in the end he decided against it. Chance based his decision partly on his father's advice. Chance was actually in the building, meeting with Sony executives, when Ken called and warned him not to sign a contract. So far, Chance had handled everything

Chance has never signed with a label, but his manager, Pat Corcoran, *left*, helps him with his career.

pretty well on his own. Maybe, Chance thought, he did not need a label.

GOING LIVE

Meanwhile, Chance's career was hurtling forward. A couple of months after *10 Day* dropped, Chance sold out Lincoln Hall, a 500-seat theater in Chicago. By the end of the year, he was tapped to be the headline act at the Metro, a club known for helping iconic bands such as Nirvana and Smashing Pumpkins gain stardom. Chance sold out two nights at the 1,100-seat venue in less than an hour.

Chance already knew how to be a rapper. Now, as *10 Day* took off, he turned his energies toward learning how to be a rap star. After seeing Chance onstage at South by Southwest, rapper Childish Gambino invited him to do a guest spot on his song "They Don't Like Me." Gambino

LIVE PERFORMANCES

Chance brings boundless energy to his live performances. He says performing live is one of his greatest talents. He credits Michael Jackson for showing him the way. As a kid, Chance watched a DVD of Jackson's *Live in Bucharest: The Dangerous Tour*. Chance studied everything from the choreography to the mood on the set, taking mental notes on how Jackson told a story and engaged the crowd. "If I hadn't gotten that DVD, I wouldn't be a live performer," Chance told *Complex*.[3]

also asked Chance to be the opening act on his 2012 tour for the album *Camp*. Gambino says their relationship is like big brother and little brother. Chance was quick to soak up Gambino's advice and expertise. For example, Chance was used to playing for smaller crowds, but Gambino taught him the skills and strategies needed to stoke up a large audience.

Chance was also hard at work on his next mixtape, *Acid Rap*. He released a couple of songs from the tape to pique the interest of his fans, and they clamored to hear more whenever they could. When Chance went to South by Southwest again in March 2013, he gave his fans what they asked for, performing the song "Juice." The song has a simple hook: "Juice! Juice! Juice!" But just in case anyone was having trouble keeping up, Chance taught

DIAL IT UP

When President Barack Obama was running for reelection in 2012, he got a little help from Chance. When Chance was eight years old, he had met Obama because Ken worked for him. Years later, after Obama had served one term as president and was running for another, Ken recognized that his son's growing fame—especially among young African Americans—could be an asset for Obama. Chance agreed and announced that he would be manning a phone bank to help the president in his reelection bid. Kids who showed up to help were rewarded with free concert tickets.

Rapper Childish Gambino helped Chance learn how to perform on the big stage.

the audience how to sing it. His energy not only lit up the crowd but even excited the jaded pros. Andrew Barber, the founder of Chicago hip-hop blog Fake Shore Drive, said, "I was walking around to the VIP area, where usually people aren't paying any attention . . . and everybody's like, 'Who's this kid?'"[4]

In the months after the release of *10 Day*, Chance was praised by critics and described as one of rap's up-and-coming stars. But plenty of artists have had successful debuts and then struggled to produce a follow-up that meets the same level of excellence. Chance was only 19. He had talent, but he was also young and relatively inexperienced. Could he do it again?

MOVING FORWARD

A year after *10 Day* came out, Chance's fans were ready for some new material. He had released a couple of songs off a new mixtape, and they had earned a good response. But people were curious about what the rest of the mixtape sounded like. Would the whole mixtape be as good as his debut had been?

TAKE TWO

Chance answered that question with a definite "yes" when he dropped *Acid Rap* in April 2013. The main theme of the tape was Chance's Chicago roots, and the response proved even more overwhelming than with his first release. Critics praised not only the music—the beats and hooks—but also the fact that Chance dug into deeper, more serious subject matter. A reviewer for the hip-hop magazine *XXL* wrote, "Ultimately, *Acid Rap*'s biggest

Chance continues to experiment with his music style.

BLESSING OR CURSE?

A visit with his grandmother, shortly after *Acid Rap* came out, helped change Chance's outlook about his life. Usually, the two just talked about lightweight stuff, but during one visit, his grandmother sat him down for a serious heart-to-heart talk. She told him she was worried about the choices he was making and that she was going to pray for him. She asked that all things not pleasing to God be taken away from Chance and "turned to dust." Later, Chance understood she just wanted him to stay on track with his life, but he admits that at first he was alarmed by her wording. "I was scared," he said on the radio show *Chicago Morning Takeover.* "[I thought] my grandma just put a voodoo curse on me!"[3]

victory is living up to its own hype."[1]

Much of the album was made while Chance was using the drug LSD, which is commonly called acid and often creates mind-altering effects. LSD is illegal in the United States. Chance says the drug's effect on him was to free his mind and jump-start his creativity. He did not regret his choice to experiment with LSD, but he acknowledged that his drug use could send the wrong message, especially to impressionable young people. When he discovered that fans had tried the drug because of his influence, Chance took steps not to glorify his drug use. "I realized the responsibility of being a popular artist," he said in a *Billboard* interview.[2]

The word *acid* in the title has another meaning as well. While making the tape, Chance listened to a lot of music called acid jazz. The distinctive sounds of this genre were a heavy influence on the tape.

Chance felt *Acid Rap* showed him maturing as an artist. His first mixtape had presented a high schooler telling a story, but this tape was more about him making music as an adult. Although it still has storytelling woven through it, at its core, *Acid Rap* focuses on music. While *10 Day* had been a complete and professional effort, it was not particularly complex—just a few tracks laid down on top of one another. *Acid Rap* was different. "With this tape, every song that was made, I was there from when the song was an idea that we were talking about, to the building of all the tracks, to the vocal and the background vocal, to deciding the features," Chance told *HipHopDX*.[4]

ACID JAZZ

Acid jazz is not the kind of music that is usually played on the radio, but it combines a lot of genres of music that are. Acid jazz thrived in the late 1980s and 1990s, but it traces its roots to music that was popular in the 1970s. While it is based in jazz, other types of music have influenced it as well, including funk, hip-hop, electronic music, soul, and even disco. Acid jazz is known for including a lot of percussion, staying close to the beat, and being repetitive, making it very danceable.

As he had with his debut, Chance produced *Acid Rap* independently. He hopped from Chicago to Los Angeles to New York, laying down tracks in home studios and getting rappers such as Childish Gambino, Action Bronson, BJ the Chicago Kid, and Twista to do guest spots. "I was just way more involved in the production side of things and making it sound the way I wanted it to sound," Chance explained to *HipHopDX*.[5]

STAYING INDEPENDENT

The buzz leading up to the release of the tape was all good, and fans were more than ready for it to drop. The record companies were back, too. Their offers were still on the table, if Chance wanted to sign. Again, he turned them down. Two weeks before he released *Acid Rap*, Chance

Chance has collaborated with a number of other artists, including Action Bronson.

acknowledged that he liked the freedom of not being tied to a major label. The release date for the tape was set, but Chance relished having ultimate control over what would happen. He could always change his mind if he wanted. He could hold it back for four more years if he wanted. "I wouldn't do that," he assured his fans in a *HipHopDX* interview.[7] But he *could*.

Chance made money by selling tickets to his concerts.

Chance released the album in the streaming-only format, which he preferred. *Acid Rap* eventually racked up more than one million downloads. Some people like something they can hold in their hands, though, and

a bootleg CD soon appeared. Despite the fact that the CD was unofficial and did not have Chance's stamp of approval, it was so popular that it climbed to the Top 100 on *Billboard* magazine's hip-hop charts.

Chance lived briefly in Hollywood Hills before moving back to Chicago.

There was some occasional controversy about his music. In the fall of 2013, Chance was slated to perform at Middlebury College in Vermont. Some students protested, however, pointing out that lyrics from "Favorite Song" on *Acid Rap* appeared to be homophobic, violating the school's community standards. Chance responded to the concerns by agreeing not to sing that lyric when he performed.

Chance still chose not to charge any money for his music. Instead, he used sites where fans could stream or download his albums for free, so that he could reach as many people as possible. Chance found other ways to generate funds. For example, he made money from ticket sales to his live shows. Merchandising was another way to bring in income. Hip-hop is not just music; it is a whole culture. As a kid, Chance had idolized Kanye West—not just his music but his whole image. Now another generation felt the same way about Chance. His image, his attitude, his style—they had value. He set up a website to sell Chance-themed merchandise, such as caps and T-shirts. Chance also found ways to save money. He traveled around in a used RV rather than spending money on nice buses or fancy hotels.

R&B singer Jeremih is one of Chance's friends.

LIFE IN LOS ANGELES

Chance had two full-length mixtapes under his belt, plus a whirlwind two years of recording and touring. By 2014, he decided to leave his Chicago home base and try somewhere new. At that point, he was not living at home anyway and was just bouncing from place to place. He decided to move to Los Angeles, California.

Chance rented a mansion in Hollywood Hills, a wealthy section of the city. The house had a pool, a movie theater, and a basketball court. Chance added a studio and recorded a song called "Wonderful Everyday." It was a cover of the theme song to the children's television program *Arthur*.

In LA, Chance hung out with other musicians, including Jeremih, BJ the Chicago Kid, and Frank Ocean. Chance dated a lot of girls, but none developed into serious relationships. For the most part, Chance just goofed around and wasted time.

While living in LA, Chance started feeling disconnected from his Chicago upbringing, especially his religious roots. He filled the void with music. One artist he really got into was Kirk Franklin, a contemporary gospel

MAKING PEACE

As the 2014 Memorial Day weekend approached, Chicago officials worried about an increase in violent crime, which tended to spike in the city during the summer. Ken knew his son's music had made him popular with the city's African Americans, who are disproportionately affected by the violence, so he asked Chance for a favor. Ken suggested he join a Twitter campaign called #SaveChicago by posting about keeping the city peaceful, at least for the weekend. Chance agreed, adding the hashtag #putYourGunsdown. For nearly two days there were no shootings. It was a small success in a city where violence was an everyday occurrence, but it was only the start. After the no-shooting streak ended, Chance tweeted, "We had a plan. We made our stand. We won the battle. But the WAR in CHICAGO is being LOST."[8]

Chance got to perform with Kirk Franklin, a gospel singer whose music inspires him, at the 2017 Grammy Awards.

musician who has won several Grammys. At 6:00 a.m., Chance's neighbors might have wanted some peace and quiet so they could sleep, but they were out of luck. Chance was on Chicago time and wide awake. He liked to play his music loud, blasting Franklin tunes out the window and through the whole neighborhood. He felt the Christian themes of the music helped him reconnect with God. Chance also paid attention to the mechanics of the music, from pitch and tone to how Franklin chose to make the chords work together.

Meanwhile, life in Chicago continued without Chance. "I looked up and months had passed and I hadn't made enough music," he remembers. "I missed a lot of weddings and funerals."[9] Finally, he admitted to himself, "[Los Angeles] wasn't where I was supposed to be."[10]

Chance decided to return to Chicago and refocus his life.

"There's not a record [Chance] can't hop on, a genre of music he can't relate to. I don't know too many people who could go on Jimmy Fallon one night and go to a peace rally the next day."[11]
—Chicago R&B singer Jeremih

READY TO EXPERIMENT

When Chance returned to Chicago, he felt a renewed faith in God and a renewed dedication to his life. He committed himself to his music, his relationships, and his hometown. His priorities showed in his work habits as well as in the themes he was expressing in his music. There were the beginnings of a new, full-length project in him, but first, he wanted to try some other things.

SURF

Artists in the Chicago music community tend to know one another and form bonds. They are usually happy to lend their talents to one another's projects, whether that means singing or shooting videos. Although Chance was climbing the ladder of a successful solo career, he remained keenly aware of his roots.

Chance describes having a daughter as life-changing.

Rap is known for being competitive—think two rappers dueling it out in a battle of words—but Chance did not buy into that. He did not care about being better than other musicians. He just cared about making the best music possible. In 2015, he decided the way to do that was to join forces with some other Chicago musicians to form a jazz-soul group called the Social Experiment.

GO FOR BROKE

Chance may give his music away for free, but making it does not come cheap. Musicians must be paid. Studios are expensive. Travel costs add up. Chance went broke making *Surf*, pouring everything he had into producing the album and then into touring with the band. Chance grew a little worried with all the expenses, but he relaxed when money started coming back in a few weeks after the album dropped, and everything turned out okay.

At the head of the Social Experiment is Nico Segal. Segal is a buddy of Chance's who plays the trumpet and goes by the stage name "Donnie Trumpet," having adopted the moniker before Donald Trump became president. Other members of the group include producer and engineer Nate Fox, composer and keyboardist Peter Cottontale (his real name is Peter Wilkins), and drummer Greg "Stix" Landfair Jr.

Nico Segal, also known as Donnie Trumpet, is one of the band members of the Social Experiment.

The group worked together on an album called *Surf.* Chance not only wrote music and rapped but also codirected the video for "Sunday Candy," the album's standout song. All the songs tap into the talents of multiple people. One song had 610 tracks to

"[Chicago rappers] got all the same fans in the city. We're playing the same venues. Musically, our sounds are different, but we really need each other in order to exist. We need the idea that rapping is important for people to help us to continue to thrive."[1]

–Chance the Rapper, speaking with Fader *in 2015*

Chance's work on *Surf* helped the project reach more than 600,000 downloads in the first week of its release on iTunes.

"The most incredible thing is that Chance is so open to whatever everyone else thinks. He's willing to put in all of his resources, all of his cards, everything on the table to make it work."[2]

—*The Social Experiment bandmate Nate Fox in a 2015 interview with* Fader

manage. The song got so complicated that the crew had to uproot themselves from Chicago and fly to a studio in Los Angeles that had better equipment just so they could finish it.

While working on *Surf*, Chance loved the idea of just being Chance, without "the Rapper" tacked on at the end. Shedding his "title" gave him some freedom. "That's what I've always wanted to do—work with my favorite writers and make something from scratch with them that we can feel like didn't exist before we came in the room," he said in a *Rolling Stone* interview.[3]

Chance concentrated on a sound that included gospel and a lot of harmony. He threw his creative efforts into coming up with interesting vocal arrangements. Rather than being responsible for carrying the lead vocals on every song, in some cases he sang only the hook, making a statement with just a few words. In "Wanna Be Cool," for example, he sings, "I don't wanna be cool, I just wanna be me."[4] As a young

NO SLACK

Chance used his musical connections to attract other artists to do guest vocals on *Surf*, but that did not always save him much work. On the song "Rememory," for instance, Chance worked with singer Erykah Badu, who is known for fusing soul, jazz, and hip-hop in her musical style. Chance acknowledges that Badu is perfectly capable of writing her own material, but this time she called on Chance to write her part of the song. If he tried to slack off or sneak out of the studio for a break, "She told me to sit my a** down and finish the piece," he recalled in a *Rolling Stone* interview.[5]

SOME HAT HISTORY

The members of the Social Experiment had a shorthand version of their name, SoX. That matched up nicely with another Chicago institution, the baseball team the Chicago White Sox. Chance approached the management of the White Sox and pointed out the similarity in the names. He liked to wear a Sox baseball cap, so he asked if they would offer him a sponsorship— paying him to wear it. The White Sox management turned him down. Maybe later, they said. A year or so passed, and the baseball team still had not offered Chance any kind of deal, so he decided it was time to switch up his look— and his now-famous 3 hat was it.

black man in America, he thinks that is an important message for kids to hear.

Surf was a success. The music magazine *Rolling Stone*, compiling lists of 2015's best albums, put it at number four for best rap albums and number 24 for all albums.

BRANCHING OUT

Surf came out in May, and soon Chance had another collaboration to share with the world. In August, he and the rapper Lil B introduced a six-track compilation called *Free.* The two musicians switch back and forth as they freestyle the verses, and Chance acknowledges at the beginning of the second track that listeners might be confused about the project's intent. Chance said the compilation let their creative juices flow to see what would result. "We're making an entire piece of content from scratch," he explained. "The best things in life come from nothing and become something different."[6]

Chance also decided to explore acting, debuting in the short film *Mr. Happy*. The film's title is misleading. The plot tells the story of a depressed man who is tired of his dead-end life and wants to commit suicide. He cannot get up the nerve to do it, so he heads to the Internet, where he hires someone to do it for him. Despite the movie's dark premise, Chance loved the script. While it may seem like a strange pairing for someone who is happy in real life, Chance hit all the right notes to make the character believable, according to director Colin Tilley.

By the end of the year, Chance was working on a dream collaboration, this time with his idol, Kanye West. When West invited

CHANCE ON SATURDAY NIGHT

Since it launched in 1975 on NBC, *Saturday Night Live* has helped define popular culture and entertainment. It is known for launching the careers of young comedians such as Eddie Murphy and Tina Fey. The show's musical guests are just as well-known. Kanye West, Frank Ocean, and Run-D.M.C. have been tapped for performances, so it was a big deal when Chance was invited to take the *SNL* stage in December 2015. He premiered the song "Somewhere in Paradise" with R&B singer Jeremih and also sang "Sunday Candy." He became the first unsigned artist to perform on the show and was invited back to *SNL* in 2016 to perform again.

Kanye West and Chance perform together at the Magnificent Coloring Day Festival in Chicago.

Chance to be on his upcoming album *The Life of Pablo*, Chance eagerly accepted. Eventually, Chance contributed to five songs on the album, including "Ultralight Beam," "Waves," "Famous," "Feedback," and "Father Stretch My Hands Pt. 1."

Chance was branching out, trying other forms of art and collaborating with various people. In the background, a new project was percolating in his mind. He did not reveal too many details, but it was not a secret, either. In fact, he had an advertisement for it on his baseball cap, which he always wore. There was no fancy logo on the hat, just the number 3. When people asked what the number referred to, Chance answered that he was working on his third major solo project. The project had a working title—*The Magnificent Coloring Book*—but that was just too many words to put on a hat.

Chance and his girlfriend, Kirsten Corley, attend a Chicago Bulls game in 2017.

GROWING UP

Early in 2015, Chance received another surprise when his girlfriend, Kirsten Corley, became pregnant. The couple welcomed a daughter, Kensli, in September. Chance promptly got a "World's Best Dad" coffee mug and the urge to talk about Kensli whenever he could. Becoming a father had a profound effect on how he viewed his life. At first, he was afraid of the impact a child would have on his lifestyle, but he soon learned to adjust. "It didn't refresh my life; it started my life," he told news anchor Katie Couric.[7] Now, everything he did became more important. Every decision went through a filter—how would his choice affect Kensli? He became much more aware of his schedule. Knowing that his daughter needed him, Chance became more efficient in how he used his time.

Chance wears his 3 hat while performing at the 2017 BET Awards.

Chance had picked the number 3 for his baseball cap to indicate that he was working on his third project, but the number gained more significance as his priorities began to crystallize. The 3 also represented the Holy Trinity of Christianity—the Father, the Son, and the Holy Ghost—which became a central theme for his next mixtape. It also represented his three-pronged family: himself, his girlfriend, and his daughter.

> "I sleep in this hat. I take showers in this hat. It doesn't come off—AT ALL!"[9]
> –Chance, during an interview with Katie Couric on February 28, 2017

By his early 20s, Chance felt as if he was growing into his own person. He was less sheltered and protected by his parents. Still, he knew he could always turn to them for advice. Becoming a father himself, Chance learned to appreciate his parents even more. "My dad's the man. And I can't say that enough," Chance said in a GQ interview. "He's always been a good dude. That's who I want to be. I'm okay if the story seems boring to people because I'm a good guy. I'm cool with that. I'd be cool with people remembering me as a good, boring dude. As long as people say good."[8]

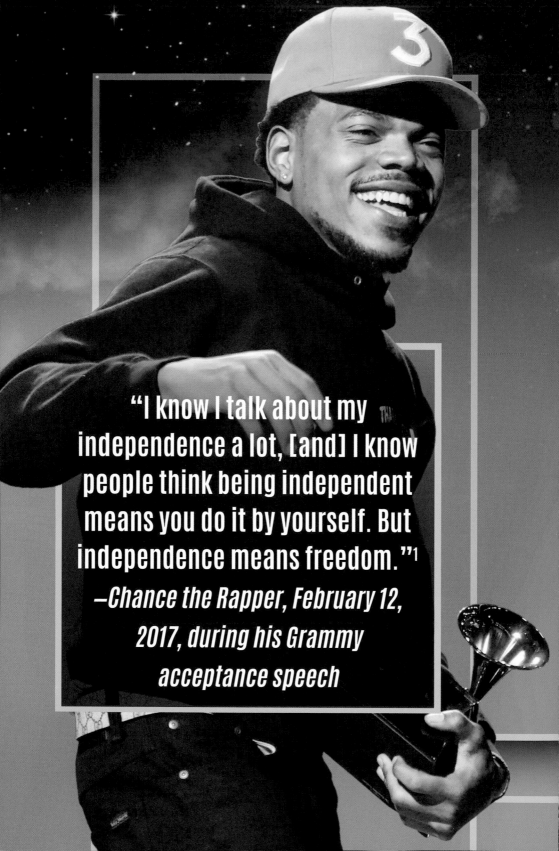

"I know I talk about my independence a lot, [and] I know people think being independent means you do it by yourself. But independence means freedom."[1]
—*Chance the Rapper, February 12, 2017, during his Grammy acceptance speech*

COLORING BOOK

Chance had early success with *10 Day* and the follow-up smash *Acid Rap*. He defied expectations when he decided not to work on another solo project right away, instead devoting his time to the Social Experiment and guest appearances on other artists' works. By 2016, more than three years had passed since his fans had heard something just from him—but he was about to give them what they wanted.

THIRD TIME IS THE CHARM

Chance's earliest thoughts on his third mixtape, *Coloring Book*, had started back when he lived in Los Angeles. He had been working on the mixtape sporadically since then. The relaxed pace gave him time to let it develop naturally, and his life experiences during this period influenced the album heavily. His Christian beliefs, his relationship with God, and the maturity that came with fatherhood all are represented. *Coloring Book* emerged as a kind of gospel rap album celebrating faith and family. One reviewer

Chance accepts the award for Best Rap Performance at the 59th annual Grammy Awards.

wrote, "[The music is] personal and panoramic, full of conversations with God, defying hip-hop norms while respecting them, proving that the genre can still dig deeper into its roots."[2]

To make the album, Chance applied some of the lessons he had learned while working with Kanye West a few months earlier on *The Life of Pablo*. Taking note of how West had used an entire studio—not just one or two rooms—to record *Pablo*, Chance rented a whole facility to record *Coloring Book*. As the project expanded, he brought in more musicians and more producers. He used an orchestra and a full choir. Everyone was working so hard that going home did not make sense. Many of the people working on the project camped out at the facility until the tape was finished, working around the clock and crashing

COVER SHOT

Bright, primary colors are just what you would expect on the cover of an album called *Coloring Book*. Chance asked the graphic designer he had worked with on *10 Day* and *Acid Rap* to go with a base color of blue for his new album—Chance's favorite color—and add a lot of red for contrast. The final cover is striking, but the colors are only one element that stands out. The cover features Chance sporting a big smile. Chance realized his best smile is the one he wears when he holds his daughter, so he and his team arranged a photo shoot to capture that smile.

on air mattresses when they needed sleep. And just as West had given Chance the opportunity to work on *Pablo,* Chance returned the favor, inviting West to guest on the opening track, "All We Got."

For *Coloring Book,* Chance still held firm to his decision not to have a record label backing him. He did, however, make a change in his marketing strategy. This time, he partnered with Apple Music, streaming *Coloring Book* free through its service exclusively for two weeks. *Coloring Book* became the first streaming-only release to make *Billboard's* Top 200 list, debuting at number eight. Carl Chery, the head of hip-hop music for Apple, raved about Chance in a *Billboard* article, saying, "This guy is the future. He's the most exciting hip-hop artist of the last five years."[3]

MAKING WAVES

Fans were clamoring for the release of Kanye West's *The Life of Pablo* in early 2016, but the project was still under wraps. It was not West's fault, though—it was Chance's. West took to Twitter to good-naturedly blame the delay on Chance. The problem, West said, was that Chance decided to lobby for a last-minute addition to the album, the song "Waves." Chance responded by tweeting back a snapshot of the album's song list, where he had sandwiched in "Waves" between the ninth and tenth tracks. The picture said it all—the song was going to be included. Chance pulled an all-nighter to finish it, tweeting afterward, "The world is better because of it."[4]

THE GREATEST TRIBUTE

Boxer Muhammad Ali died in June 2016. He was a hero to many people, especially in the African-American community. Chance was honored when he was asked to give a tribute to Ali at the ESPYs, a sports awards show. Chance wrote a new song for the occasion and started playing around with lyrics just four days before the show. First he tried writing boxing metaphors, but he decided they were too cheesy. Next he tried framing the song as a letter from his mother, who was a big Ali fan. That did not work either. Ultimately, the song took on a gospel flavor, celebrating the parallels Chance saw between his own dad and Ali. The lyrics said, "I was a rock, I was a rock and roller/Back in my day/But now I'm just a rock."[5]

GRAMMY TIME

"OMG six!" That was the text that Chance got from his manager, Pat Corcoran, one morning in early December 2016. The nominations had just been announced for the Grammys, the premier awards show for popular music, which would be held in February 2017.

Despite the critical and popular appeal of *Coloring Book*, Corcoran had feared Chance would not be recognized by the Recording Academy, which sponsors the Grammys. He and Chance had not done things the traditional way, after all. It was unusual enough that Chance was taking the music world by storm as an unsigned, independent artist. So Corcoran was

With Muhammad Ali pictured on-screen, Chance performs at the 2016 ESPY Awards.

ecstatic when Chance received six nominations. However, Corcoran was not paying close enough attention. Chance returned a one-word text to set the record straight: "Seven."[6]

The seven nominations came in various categories, including Best New Artist, Best Rap Performance, Best Rap Album, and Best Rap Song. Only a few months earlier, Chance's odds to receive a nomination were much lower, based on how the Grammys were structured. Since the awards show began in 1959, only artists who had released their material physically—an actual record, tape, or CD—were eligible for nominations. A spokesperson for the Grammys said the reason for that was based on practicalities. Even just counting physical products, the voters have to sift through about 23,000 releases per year. Adding streaming-only releases could increase the number so much it might be unrealistic to get through all the material.

So, as a streaming-only release, *Coloring Book* was out of the running. But few albums had received the kind of attention that *Coloring Book* had. It was widely hailed as one of the year's best. If the point of the Grammys was to recognize and reward good music, how could the Academy ignore it?

THE RULE CHANGE

The music business was changing, though, and Chance was in the right place at the right time. Shortly before the nominations came out, the Academy announced it was changing its rules to let streaming-only albums be included for consideration. The rule change came during the same year that *Coloring Book* was released, so it seemed as if Chance had actually been the reason behind the change—especially since he had personally lobbied for it. However, an Academy spokesman said that was just a coincidence. Streaming sites were becoming more and more popular with listeners, and the music available on them was getting more attention. The new rule change was put into place to reflect that. David Bakula works with Nielsen Entertainment, a company that collects statistics and studies trends in the entertainment industry.

"Streaming is changing the way artists release albums and [is] changing the album as an art form," he noted in a *Rolling Stone* article. "Streaming is putting life back in the music catalog."[7]

On February 12, 2017, Chance attended the Grammys and performed a medley of songs from *Coloring Book*, including "All We Got" and "Blessings." Also in the medley was "How Great," a gospel song

CHANCE'S OTHER DAD

Kevin Coval, a Chicago poet and educator, mentored Chance as a teenager and helped him get *10 Day* off the ground. Coval released a new volume of poetry in 2017, *The People's History of Chicago*, and recruited Chance to write the book's foreword. In it, Chance calls Coval his "artistic father," saying Coval taught him how to make his art into a job. "He made me understand what it is to be a poet, what it is to be an artist, and what it is to serve the people," Chance said.[8]

that Chance says is his favorite from the mixtape. When the winners were announced, Chance proved himself big-time. He won in the categories of Best New Artist, Best Rap Performance for his song "No Problem," and Best Rap Album for *Coloring Book*.

Dressed in a gray suit and tie—and a matching gray 3 hat—Chance took the stage to accept his Best Rap Album award. He told the crowd that he did not have a speech prepared because he had not expected to win the award. But he had plenty to say. After thanking God, his family, and his friends, Chance announced that the award was for "every independent artist" trying to do the same thing he was.[9] Chance's speech started off subdued, but he got more excited as he continued. By the end of the speech, he was joyfully shouting with enthusiasm, hands in the air. And his 3 hat gained another meaning: three Grammy wins.

HOMETOWN HERO

Chicago may be the third-largest city in the United States, but to Chance, it still feels like a small town. He was born and raised in Chicago and knows the city inside and out. Like most Chicagoans, Chance has an opinion about pizza—he calls his favorite, from Lou Malnati's, the "best food on Earth."[1] He is also a devoted Chicago Bulls fan. And if he wants to catch some good, new hip-hop music, he heads to the Shrine in the South Loop. To Chance, the city is like a fishbowl. He told *ESPN The Magazine*, "I've swam around a bunch of times."[2] And if he has his way, he will be swimming around a lot more.

THE FACES OF CHICAGO

The level of violent crime in Chicago ranks among the highest in the nation. For Chicago natives who love their city, that is an especially sad fact to face. Chance bristles

Chance throws the ceremonial first pitch at a Chicago White Sox game.

CHICKEN OUT

Pizza. Doughnuts. Barbecue. Native Chicagoans love to talk about the best food and where to get it. When the conversation turns to chicken, Chance thinks nowhere beats the local chain Harold's Chicken Shack. There is one just a few streets away from his home, and Chance is known to order up the six-wing dinner with hot sauce and lemon pepper, along with a sweet tea to drink. For his twenty-fourth birthday, Chance even got a cake with a Harold's theme, decorated with the restaurant's logo and featuring frosting versions of chicken wings and fries spilling off the top.

when people disparage the city or discuss its problems in an insensitive way. In 2015, filmmaker Spike Lee released the movie *Chi-Raq*, which documented the violence in Chicago. (The movie title combines the names "Chicago" and "Iraq," because the Middle Eastern nation is a war-torn country.) Chance did not like the movie, and he made his thoughts clear in a series of tweets that blasted the film. He thought the way Lee handled the problem was offensive and that it minimized the heartache of Chicagoans touched by violence. The feud continued when Lee responded by calling Chance a fraud, saying that Chance was not acknowledging the extent of the problem.

Chance does not deny the city has problems, but he points out that they do not reflect all of Chicago or what it has to offer. The city has a vibrant cultural scene and a healthy business and development climate, for instance. But where the problems are greatest, Chance notes that the burden falls hardest on minorities. Turning things around will take a number of efforts, from improving relations with law enforcement officers to devoting more money to schools and affordable housing. Perhaps most important, Chance understands that fear about the situation affects all Chicagoans, regardless of their skin color or wealth. In "Paranoia," a bonus track from *Acid Rap*, Chance raps, "We know you're scared. You should ask us if we're scared too."[3]

ARTIST AND ACTIVIST

Celebrities often take the stage not just as performers but as activists. Their fame puts them in a good position to promote causes that are important to them.

THAT'S FUNNY, RIGHT?

In addition to its music community, Chicago also boasts a thriving comedy scene. Once, Chance went to see a friend perform. As showtime neared, however, his friend developed a bad case of stage fright—he did not think his jokes were any good. To encourage him, Chance offered a dare: if his friend went onstage, so would he. His friend agreed, and the two spent the next half hour writing new material. Chance ended up with about 30 one-liners that amounted to a seven-minute monologue.

Chance's music already has an underlying political theme to it, because he often raps about Chicago—the good and the bad. But he is also willing to tackle the city's problems head-on, backing up his words with actions. Interviewed for a session about activism at the Institute of Politics at the University of Chicago, Chance said, "I think I'm as vocal as I'm supposed to be at times, and as physical as I'm supposed to be at times." He went on to put it another way: "There's a time to be outside in the streets, and there's a time to be outside in the tweets!"[4]

From the time his dad volunteered him to help the neighbors with their chores, Chance has felt a duty to be a productive member of his community. It started with the few blocks that radiated out from his home, but now Chance feels a responsibility to the entire city.

ON THE FIELD

Shortly after Chance released *Coloring Book*, he announced he would tour to promote it. The flagship event was a festival held right in Chance's backyard, on Chicago's South Side at US Cellular Field, where the White Sox baseball team plays. The event was clearly aimed at Chicago's youth and Chance's core base of fans. Tickets were relatively cheap, and Chance was proud of the fact the festival also created jobs for African Americans in the area. Approximately 50,000 people turned out—breaking an attendance record at the park. It was his way to say thank you to everyone who had helped make his career.

Chicago's winter days average 26.4 degrees Fahrenheit (-3.1°C), making warm clothing very important.

One project he is involved with is called Warmest Winter. The bitterly cold winters in Chicago can be especially tough for the city's homeless people, so Chance helped promote a combination coat and sleeping bag—made by homeless people—to be distributed to the city's most vulnerable.

Chance took a more active interest in politics as the country geared up for the 2016 presidential election. Historically, young adults are among those least likely to vote. Chance wanted to encourage them to have a voice, so he organized an event called Parade to the Polls. He threw a free concert in Grant Park, and afterward

After the presidential election was over, Chance sang "Jingle Bells" with Santa Claus and President Barack Obama in early December 2016.

"[Kids] trust me and they understand my views. . . . I can't necessarily save everybody that's my age, because people gotta make their own choices, . . . but I can't worry about what my contemporaries are doing. I have to worry about, you know, the future of Chicago."[5]

—Chance the Rapper

the crowd marched to a polling place to cast their ballots during early voting. Approximately 6,000 people participated.

THE NEXT GENERATION

In 2014, Chance was voted "Outstanding Youth of the Year" by Chicago's young people, and his popularity has not eased up. Helping the next generation is one of Chance's top priorities. He knows firsthand how much of a difference it can make for young people to have opportunities to express themselves. To give back, Chance started a program called Social Works, which is devoted to offering artistic, educational, and civic opportunities to Chicago's kids. Chance hopes that giving kids something to work on, and something to care about, will deter them from violence. "You don't have any respect for life—or respect for anyone else's life—if you don't have anything going on," he reasoned in a *Billboard* interview.[6]

Chance also likes to just hang out with kids. One time, he showed up at a day camp and accompanied some elementary-age children on a trip to the Field Museum. A video filmed on the bus ride there confirms the kids thought

BACK TO CLASS

Chance used to welcome getting out of class, but now he is trying to help kids succeed in school. In 2015, he and his brother, Taylor, helped raise $100,000 to bring new technology into Chicago's elementary schools. Then, in 2017, Chance donated $1 million to the city's public school system. Afterward, three sophomores at Lake View High School wrote him a thank-you letter. In it, they said, "We look up to you because the fame usually takes humility away from artists, but it hasn't changed you. . . . You're using your fame for good and not just to look good."[7]

Chance feels a great responsibility to give back to his community, including the public school system in Chicago.

he was a pretty cool chaperone. It was not long before he had everyone chanting, "Field trip! Field trip!"[8]

"I feel a certain duty to Chicago, and to my family that lives here, and to the people I grew up with that live here, and to people I don't know that live here," Chance

told Katie Couric in a 2017 interview. "I'm a plant. If you uproot a plant and put that somewhere else, it's not going to grow the same. This is where I'm supposed to be, and where I'm supposed to grow and figure out what I'm supposed to be."[9]

LEGACY

The high that came from three Grammys did not last long. Chance left the stage, he got his picture taken with his awards, and then it was over. It felt like a letdown, but Chance did not stay down for long. Even though he had wanted a Grammy his whole life, he knew he had to put everything in perspective. Winning the Grammys was just one stop on his journey, not the final destination. Now, it was time to turn his attention to whatever came next.

NEXT STEPS

Just a week after the Grammys, Chance teased his fans on Instagram with two short videos. They showed him and fellow rap artist Future in a studio, running through a song. Chance did not offer too many details about the piano-heavy track, but he included the hashtag #MyPeak, which references a line in the song and was presumably the title. His fans were glad to see it. Chance was back making music. A few months later, he was also earning

Chance the Rapper won the Best New Artist and Humanitarian awards at the 2017 BET Awards.

BEST RAPPER ALIVE

Chance was named Best Rapper Alive by *Complex* magazine for his work in 2016. The magazine recognized that Chance set new trends in rap. He does not write resentful raps about what he wants or what he has been denied. Instead, he creates positive, Christian-based lyrics celebrating his family and other blessings. While his approach is different in the world of rap, it works for Chance.

Chance finds himself in good company in earning the honor. Kanye West won in 2010. Drake reigns as a three-time winner—2011, 2012, and 2015.

more awards, receiving the Best New Artist and the Humanitarian awards from BET (Black Entertainment Television) in June 2017.

Chance also revealed that he was considering making some more major changes in his approach to his music, both creatively and on the business side. For one thing, instead of a mixtape, he said his next release might be an album. Those two words are often used to mean the same thing, but Chance sees a definite difference. To him, an album has more of a story line and a strong visual element. "When I'm making music usually, I'm writing it because I want you to listen in the car, and I'm also thinking of the day we finally meet and I get to play it for you," he said in an interview with *Pitchfork*.[1] With that in mind, he wants his album to have a live show to go with it.

Even more notably, he said his next release might not be free. The reason was not because he needed to make more money. Instead, it had to do with how the music business is set up. Streaming-only songs, the format Chance prefers, had big odds to overcome. According to music industry regulations, free streaming music is not treated the same as songs or albums that are purchased the traditional way. Instead, a free song must be streamed about 1,500 times to count as a single sale. Chance argues that no one listens to a song—even a great one—1,500 times after they buy it.

The way people get access to his music does not make him less popular, but it *does* make that popularity harder to measure. Being counted at a ratio of 1,500-to-1 means it is much harder to end up on charts that rank the most

COMMON KNOWLEDGE

In 2017, *Time* magazine named Chance to its list of 100 Most Influential People. As a tribute, fellow rapper Common remembered a time he reached out to Chance as a kid. Common is also from Chicago, and his grandmother asked him to call her friend's grandson—Chance—and give him some advice on becoming a rapper. Common agreed, saying, "I told him to keep following his dreams. Then I forgot all about it." Chance did not forget. Years later, when the two met, Chance told him, "You won't remember this, but you called me when I was a kid."[2]

Chance remembers receiving encouragement from rapper Common when he was just a kid.

successful songs or albums. For example, Chance racked up 38,000 "equivalent album units" for *Coloring Book*, because the tape got more than 57 million streams. Those

levels are difficult to reach all the time, though. Chance does not like being kept off the charts, so one solution is to switch up how he releases his music.

> "I think it's always the job of the artist, in trying times or not—it's always our job to tell the truth."[3]
>
> —*Chance the Rapper*

RECIPE FOR SUCCESS

Part of Chance's streaming success comes from good timing. When he released *10 Day*, a lot of social media and user-producer sites were getting more popular. Twitter was moving into the mainstream. People were learning how to use sharing sites such as SoundCloud and YouTube. Chance had a good understanding of how to use these new outlets. Social media also let Chance capitalize on his friendly personality, lending a personal touch by communicating with fans through tweets or other posts. In turn, fans might post pictures or stories of their own experiences with the rapper, helping his reputation spread.

Of course, Chance could not make money if all he did was give away his music for free. But he could build on the goodwill that he generated by offering free music. His fan base grew, and those fans rewarded his efforts by buying tickets to his shows and merchandise from his website.

Independence from a record label also allowed Chance the freedom to record and release what he wanted, when he wanted. With no pressure to turn out a certain amount of music by a certain deadline, Chance pursued only the projects that interested him and worked according to his own schedule. His third album, *Coloring Book*, came three years after his previous one—a long time in the music industry. But its quality proved it was worth the wait, and Chance's reputation was bolstered as a result.

Of course, Chance did not single-handedly change how the recording industry works. Certainly, there were independent artists before him. And lots of musicians have used the far-reaching, free platform of the Internet to promote their music. But he was among the first to recognize how to harness it the most effectively.

THE *HAMILTON* MIXTAPE

Chance was a big fan of the musical *Hamilton*, which took Broadway by storm in 2015. The show's musical score includes a lot of rap songs, taking a different approach from most musical theater shows. The musical, which is about Alexander Hamilton, one of America's founding fathers, won multiple awards after its debut. In 2016, another *Hamilton*-themed project came out called *The Hamilton Mixtape*, which includes covers of the songs from the show. Chance contributes to "Dear Theodosia," his favorite piece from the musical.

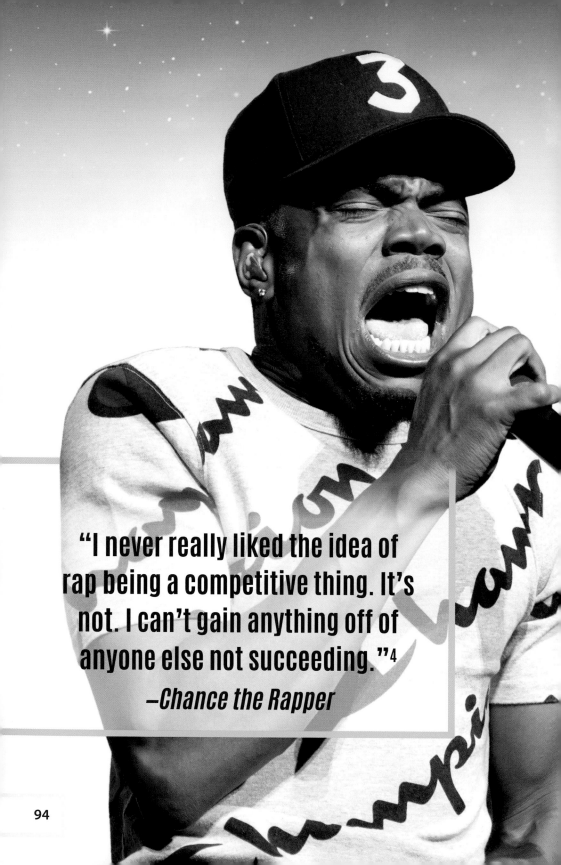

"I never really liked the idea of rap being a competitive thing. It's not. I can't gain anything off of anyone else not succeeding."[4]
—Chance the Rapper

LEAVING IT TO CHANCE

It took Chance just five years to go from being a floundering high school senior, unsure of his future, to a rapper on the verge of superstardom. Along the way, he has not followed the conventional path.

In the early 2010s, Chicago drill rap emerged. This new style was a turn into darker territory, reflecting the city's violence. Chance responded by keeping things joyful, bringing his religious faith to the forefront. When many artists would have traded some of their creative freedom for the security of a record deal, Chance stayed independent. His choices have paid off. He has earned critical acclaim for his music, financial rewards, the devotion of a growing fan base, and a wide-open future. During a session at the University of Chicago's Institute of Politics, he was asked, "Is there anything that Chance can't do?" Chance replied, "Yes, there is one thing I can't do, and that's *fail*!"[5]

He was joking, but it seems pretty close to the truth. And even though Chance does not have to be humble, he often is. "I am still a kid, and am still growing," he told

Chance's star was still rising as he performed to a packed crowd at the Lollapalooza music festival in Chicago in August 2017.

Zane Lowe. "I still don't fully understand how everything works and my potential and what I'm going to do."[6]

What he does understand is that he has rightfully earned the accomplishments he has made up to now. He took the right steps at the right time. He believes in the power of two things: God and hard work.

Artists often get the advice *not* to leave everything to chance. But for this young Chicago star, believing in Chance was the best thing he could have done.

CHANCE THE ACTOR

Delivering pizza does not sound like a dangerous job, but it gets pretty dicey in *Slice*, a movie filmed in 2016, that is part horror, part comedy. Chance stars in the film as Dax Lycander, a mysterious outlaw (who also happens to be a werewolf) who is accused of killing pizza delivery boys. The film was written and directed by Austin Vesely, Chance's friend and longtime collaborator for music videos. Vesely originally planned to adjust the role to suit Chance's personality, but he says the rapper turned out to be such a good actor that he did not have to change much.

TIMELINE

1993
Chancelor Bennett is born in Chicago, Illinois.

2001
Chance decides to become a rapper.

2004
Kanye West releases *The College Dropout*, the first rap album Chance buys.

2007
Chance teams up with two friends during his first shot at recording in a cousin's studio.

2009
YouMedia, an open-mic venue, opens in Chicago; Chance soon becomes a regular.

2011
Chance graduates from high school and starts work on *10 Day*, his first serious effort at a mixtape.

2012
In April, Chance's first mixtape, *10 Day*, is released; Chance goes on tour with Childish Gambino.

2013

In April, *Acid Rap* is released and later is named as one of the year's best albums by several music magazines.

2014

Chance was voted Chicago's "Outstanding Youth of the Year" by the city's young people.

2015

The Social Experiment, a Chicago-based band including Chance, releases *Surf*; late-night variety TV show *Saturday Night Live* features Chance, the first unsigned artist to perform on the program; Chance and his girlfriend welcome a daughter, Kensli.

2016

Chance works with Kanye West on *The Life of Pablo*; Chance releases *Coloring Book*, his third mixtape; after the death of boxer Muhammad Ali, Chance writes a song and performs it at a tribute ceremony; *Complex* magazine names Chance "Best Rapper Alive."

2017

Chance wins Grammys for Best Rap Album, Best Rap Performance, and Best New Artist; Chance wins the BET Best New Artist and Humanitarian awards.

DATE OF BIRTH

April 16, 1993

PLACE OF BIRTH

Chicago, Illinois

PARENTS

Ken Williams-Bennett and Lisa Bennett

EDUCATION

Graduated from Jones Prep High School in 2011

CHILDREN

Daughter, Kensli, born in September 2015

CAREER HIGHLIGHTS

Chance released his first mixtape within a year of finishing high school. He went on to release two more major solo projects, one of which became the first streaming-only album ever to earn a spot on the *Billboard* charts. He has also won three Grammys, including Best New Artist, as well as the Best New Artist award from BET. He also won the BET Humanitarian award. He devotes much of his time and money to social causes that benefit the people in his hometown of Chicago.

ALBUMS

10 Day (2012); *Acid Rap* (2013); *Surf* (with The Social Experiment, 2015); *Coloring Book* (2016)

CONTRIBUTION TO HIP-HOP

Chance has pioneered a form of rap that successfully combines elements of traditional hip-hop with gospel music. He produced his first three mixtapes without the assistance of a major record label, helping to pave the way for other independent artists.

CONFLICTS

Chance angered filmmaker Spike Lee when he said Lee's movie *Chi-Raq* treated the problem of violent crime in Chicago in an offensive manner. A lyric in Chance's "Favorite Song" was perceived as being homophobic, leading some college students to protest an upcoming 2013 performance by Chance at Middlebury College in Vermont. In response, Chance agreed not to sing the lyric during his show.

QUOTE

"I know I talk about my independence a lot, [and] I know people think being independent means you do it by yourself. But independence means freedom."

—Chance the Rapper

BOOTLEG
An illegal recording.

COLLABORATION
A project that two or more people work on together.

CONTEMPORARY
A person who is about the same age as another person.

COVER
A version of a song previously performed by another artist.

DEBUT
The first album or publication by a musician or group.

DRILL
A type of rap music characterized by dark and often violent themes.

GENRE
A specific type of music, film, or writing.

HOOK
A short, catchy part of a song, often repeated.

HYPE
Excessive, exaggerated attention given to something.

MEDLEY

Parts of several songs combined to form a single piece of music.

MENTOR

Someone who offers advice and encouragement to a less-experienced person.

MONOLOGUE

A long speech made by one person.

NOMINATION

The act of suggesting a person or work for a particular award.

PANORAMIC

Including a wide array of material or viewpoints.

PERCUSSION

An instrument that keeps the beat in a song.

STREAM

To access music or videos on the Internet.

TRIBUTE

The act of honoring someone.

VENUE

A place where events are held.

SELECTED BIBLIOGRAPHY

Austen, Ben. "The New Pioneers: Chance the Rapper Is One of the Hottest Acts in Music, Has a Top 10 Album and His Own Festival—All without a Label or Physical Release." *Billboard.* Billboard. 11 Aug. 2016. Web. 4 Sept. 2017.

Green, Mark Anthony. "The Gospel According to Chance the Rapper." *GQ.* GQ. 14 Feb. 2017. Web. 4 Sept. 2017.

Nosnitsky, Andrew. "Why Chance the Rapper Is Forgoing Solo Fame to Make Jazzy Songs with Friends." *Fader.* Fader. Feb./Mar. 2015. Web. 4 Sept. 2017.

Vozick-Levinson, Simon. "Chance the Rapper Is Doing Exactly What He Wants." *Rolling Stone.* Rolling Stone. 25 June 2015. Web. 4 Sept. 2017.

FURTHER READINGS

Baker, Soren. *The History of Rap and Hip-Hop.* Detroit: Lucent, 2012. Print.

Berlatsky, Noah. *Rap Music.* Detroit: Greenhaven, 2013. Print.

Cummings, Judy Dodge. *Hip-Hop Culture.* Minneapolis: Abdo, 2017. Print.

ONLINE RESOURCES

Booklinks

NONFICTION NETWORK

FREE! ONLINE NONFICTION RESOURCES

To learn more about Chance the Rapper, visit **abdobooklinks.com**. These links are routinely monitored and updated to provide the most current information available.

MORE INFORMATION

For more information on this subject, contact or visit the following organizations:

THE HIPHOP ARCHIVE AND RESEARCH INSTITUTE
Du Bois Research Institute
Hutchins Center for African & African American Research
104 Mt. Auburn St.
Cambridge, MA 02138
617-496-8885
hiphoparchive.org

Scholars and artists join forces at HARI, established in 2002, to conduct research, preserve materials, and create programs for youth.

WORDS BEATS & LIFE INC.
1525 Newton St. NW
Washington, DC 20010
202-667-1192
wblinc.org

WBL works to empower students through a variety of educational and performing programs that promote creativity through hip-hop culture.

YOUTH SPEAKS
1663 Mission St., Ste. 604
San Francisco, CA 94103
415-255-9035
youthspeaks.org/

Founded in 1996, Youth Speaks works with young people to help them find their voices through spoken-word performances.

SOURCE NOTES

CHAPTER 1. A FATEFUL SUMMER

1. Carl Lamarre. "Chance the Rapper Talks Fatherhood, Grammy Night & Origin of His '3' Hat with Katie Couric: Watch." *Billboard*. Billboard, 28 Feb. 2017. Web. 4 Sept. 2017.

2. Leor Galil. "Chance the Rapper Drops Acid Rap." *Chicago Reader*. Sun-Times Media, 23 Apr. 2013. Web. 4 Sept. 2017.

3. DanRys. "Chance the Rapper Talks the Chicago Scene & His 'Acid Rap' Mixtape." *HipHopDX*. HipHopDX, 13 May 2013. Web. 4 Sept. 2017.

4. Ibid.

CHAPTER 2. A KID FROM CHICAGO

1. Mark Anthony Green. "The Gospel According to Chance the Rapper." *GQ*. Condé Nast, 14 Feb. 2017. Web. 4 Sept. 2017.

2. Leor Galil. "Chance the Rapper Drops Acid Rap." *Chicago Reader*. Sun-Times Media, 23 Apr. 2013. Web. 4 Sept. 2017.

3. Corban Goble. "Chance the Rapper." *Pitchfork*. Condé Nast, 23 Apr. 2013. Web. 4 Sept. 2017.

CHAPTER 3. BREAKTHROUGH

1. Jacob Shamsian and Paul Schrodt. "A 23-Year-Old Rapper Who Refuses to Sign a Record Deal Is Tearing Up the Hip-Hop World All by Himself." *Business Insider*. Business Insider, 29 Aug. 2016. Web. 4 Sept. 2017.

2. Ben Austen. "The New Pioneers: Chance the Rapper Is One of the Hottest Acts in Music, Has a Top 10 Album and His Own Festival—All Without a Label or Physical Release." *Billboard*. Billboard, 11 Aug. 2016. Web. 4 Sept. 2017.

3. David Drake. "Chance the Rapper: Acid Test (2013 Cover Story)." *Complex*. Complex Media, 13 May 2016. Web. 4 Sept. 2017.

4. Leor Galil. "Chance the Rapper Drops Acid Rap." *Chicago Reader*. Sun-Times Media, 23 Apr. 2013. Web. 4 Sept. 2017.

CHAPTER 4. MOVING FORWARD

1. "Mixtape Review: Chance the Rapper, Acid Rap." *XXL*. XXL Network, 13 May 2013. Web. 4 Sept. 2017.

2. Ben Austen. "The New Pioneers: Chance the Rapper Is One of the Hottest Acts in Music, Has a Top 10 Album and His Own Festival—All Without a Label or Physical Release." *Billboard*. Billboard, 11 Aug. 2016. Web. 4 Sept. 2017.

3. "Chance the Rapper Talks Donald Trump, Sesame Street, Soundcloud, Grammy Awards & God." *YouTube*. YouTube, 18 Nov. 2016. Web. 4 Sept. 2017.

4. DanRys. "Chance the Rapper Talks the Chicago Scene & His 'Acid Rap' Mixtape." *HipHopDX*. HipHopDX, 13 May 2013. Web. 4 Sept. 2017.

5. Ibid.

6. "Chance the Rapper with Zane Lowe." *YouTube*. YouTube, 27 Dec. 2016. Web. 7 May 2017.

7. DanRys. "Chance the Rapper Talks the Chicago Scene & His 'Acid Rap' Mixtape." *HipHopDX*. HipHopDX, 13 May 2013. Web. 4 Sept. 2017.

8. Stacy-Ann Ellis. "Chance the Rapper Helped Halt Chicago Violence for Almost Two Days." *Vibe*. Billboard-Hollywood Reporter Media Group, 29 May 2014. Web. 4 Sept. 2017.

9. Ben Austen. "The New Pioneers: Chance the Rapper Is One of the Hottest Acts in Music, Has a Top 10 Album and His Own Festival—All Without a Label or Physical Release." *Billboard*. Billboard, 11 Aug. 2016. Web. 4 Sept. 2017.

10. Zach Baron. "How Chance the Rapper's Life Became Perfect." *GQ*. Condé Nast, 24 Aug. 2016. Web. 4 Sept. 2017.

11. Ben Austen. "The New Pioneers: Chance the Rapper Is One of the Hottest Acts in Music, Has a Top 10 Album and His Own Festival—All Without a Label or Physical Release." *Billboard*. Billboard, 11 Aug. 2016. Web. 4 Sept. 2017.

CHAPTER 5. READY TO EXPERIMENT

1. Andrew Nosnitsky. "Why Chance the Rapper Is Forgoing Solo Fame to Make Jazzy Songs with Friends." *Fader*. Fader, n.d. Web. 4 Sept. 2017.

2. Ibid.

3. Simon Vozick-Levinson. "Chance the Rapper Is Doing Exactly What He Wants." *Rolling Stone*. Rolling Stone, 25 June 2015. Web. 4 Sept. 2017.

4. Ibid.

5. Ibid.

6. Barnes, Tom. "Chance the Rapper and Lil B Just Released a Surprise Album—And It's Pretty Boss." *Mic*. Mic Network, 5 Aug. 2015. Web. 4 Sept. 2017.

7. Carl Lamarre. "Chance the Rapper Talks Fatherhood, Grammy Night & Origin of His '3' Hat with Katie Couric: Watch." *Billboard*. Billboard, 28 Feb. 2017. Web. 4 Sept. 2017.

8. Mark Anthony Green. "The Gospel According to Chance the Rapper." *GQ*. Condé Nast, 14 Feb. 2017. Web. 4 Sept. 2017.

9. Carl Lamarre. "Chance the Rapper Talks Fatherhood, Grammy Night & Origin of His '3' Hat with Katie Couric: Watch." *Billboard*. Billboard, 28 Feb. 2017. Web. 4 Sept. 2017.

CHAPTER 6. COLORING BOOK

1. Jimmy Blake. "Grammys 2017: The Rise of Chance the Rapper." *BBC*. BBC, 13 Feb. 2017. Web. 4 Sept. 2017.

2. Kris Ex. "Chance the Rapper: Coloring Book." *Pitchfork*. Condé Nast, 17 May 2016. Web. 4 Sept. 2017.

3. Ben Austen. "The New Pioneers: Chance the Rapper Is One of the Hottest Acts in Music, Has a Top 10 Album and His Own Festival—All Without a Label or Physical Release." *Billboard*. Billboard, 11 Aug. 2016. Web. 4 Sept. 2017.

4. Daniel Kreps. "'Blame Chance': Kanye West Explains 'Life of Pablo' Album Delay." *Rolling Stone*. Rolling Stone, 13 Feb. 2016. Web. 4 Sept. 2017.

5. Ben Austen. "The New Pioneers: Chance the Rapper Is One of the Hottest Acts in Music, Has a Top 10 Album and His Own Festival—All Without a Label or Physical Release." *Billboard*. Billboard, 11 Aug. 2016. Web. 4 Sept. 2017.

6. Rebecca Haithcoat. "Chance the Rapper's Manager on Steering Clear of Major Labels & Still Scoring 7 Grammy Noms." *Billboard*. Billboard, 2 Feb. 2017. Web. 4 Sept. 2017.

7. Sarah Grant. "What Chance the Rapper's Streaming-Only Grammy Nod Means for Pop's Future." *Rolling Stone*. Rolling Stone, 10 Feb. 2017. Web. 4 Sept. 2017.

8. Justin Ivey. "Chance the Rapper Writes Foreword for New Poetry Book." *XXL*. XXL Network, 3 Mar. 2017. Web. 4 Sept. 2017.

9. "Chance the Rapper Wins Best Rap Album GRAMMY." *Recording Academy*. Recording Academy, n.d. Web. 4 Sept. 2017.

CHAPTER 7. HOMETOWN HERO

1. "Chance the Rapper Reddit AMA Reveals Star's Pizza Love, Dream Partner and a Billy Dee Williams Connection." *HuffPost*. Oath, 2 Aug. 2013. Web. 4 Sept. 2017.

2. Justin Tinsley. "No Labels: Chance the Rapper and Jimmy Butler." *Undefeated*. ESPN Internet Ventures, n.d. Web. 25 Sept. 2017.

3. Andrew Nosnitsky. "Why Chance the Rapper Is Forgoing Solo Fame to Make Jazzy Songs with Friends." *Fader*. Fader, n.d. Web. 4 Sept. 2017.

4. "Chance the Rapper and the Art of Activism." *YouTube*. YouTube, 1 June 2016. Web. 4 Sept. 2017.

5. Kevin Goddard. "Chance the Rapper Talks New Music, Fatherhood, Politics, & More on Hot 97." *Hot New Hip Hop*. Urbanlinx, 24 Oct. 2015. Web. 26 Oct. 2017.

6. Carl Lamarre. "Chance the Rapper Talks Fatherhood, Grammy Night & Origin of His '3' Hat with Katie Couric: Watch." *Billboard*. Billboard, 28 Feb. 2017. Web. 4 Sept. 2017.

7. Alex Rojas, Alondra Cerros, and Annelisse Betancourt. "An Open Letter to Chance the Rapper from Chicago Students: 'You're More Than Just an Artist to Us, You Are a Way of Life.'" *Billboard*. Billboard, 15 Mar. 2017. Web. 4 Sept. 2017.

8. Zach Frydenlund. "Chance the Rapper Surprised Some Chicago Kids with a Field Trip to a Museum Today." *Complex*. Complex Media, 7 July 2015. Web. 4 Sept. 2017.

9. Carl Lamarre. "Chance the Rapper Talks Fatherhood, Grammy Night & Origin of His '3' Hat with Katie Couric: Watch." *Billboard*. Billboard, 28 Feb. 2017. Web. 4 Sept. 2017.

CHAPTER 8. LEGACY

1. Kevin Lozano. "Chance the Rapper Is Working on His Debut Album." *Pitchfork*. Condé Nast, 23 Nov. 2016. Web. 4 Sept. 2017.

2. Adelle Platon. "Common Recalls the Time He Gave Advice to a Young Rapper Who Turned Out to Be Chance the Rapper." *Billboard*. Billboard, 20 Apr. 2017. Web. 4 Sept. 2017.

3. Zach Baron. "How Chance the Rapper's Life Became Perfect." *GQ*. Condé Nast, 24 Aug. 2016. Web. 4 Sept. 2017.

4. Ben Austen. "The New Pioneers: Chance the Rapper Is One of the Hottest Acts in Music, Has a Top 10 Album and His Own Festival—All Without a Label or Physical Release." *Billboard*. Billboard, 11 Aug. 2016. Web. 4 Sept. 2017.

5. "Chance the Rapper and the Art of Activism." *YouTube*. YouTube, 1 June 2016. Web. 4 Sept. 2017.

6. "Chance the Rapper with Zane Lowe." *YouTube*. YouTube, 27 Dec. 2016. Web. 7 May 2017.

Diane Bailey has written dozens of nonfiction books for kids and teens on topics including sports, the environment, animals, and careers. Her favorite is anything to do with history, from ancient Greece on up to the twentieth century. She has two sons and lives in Kansas.